ROBOT SCIENTIST

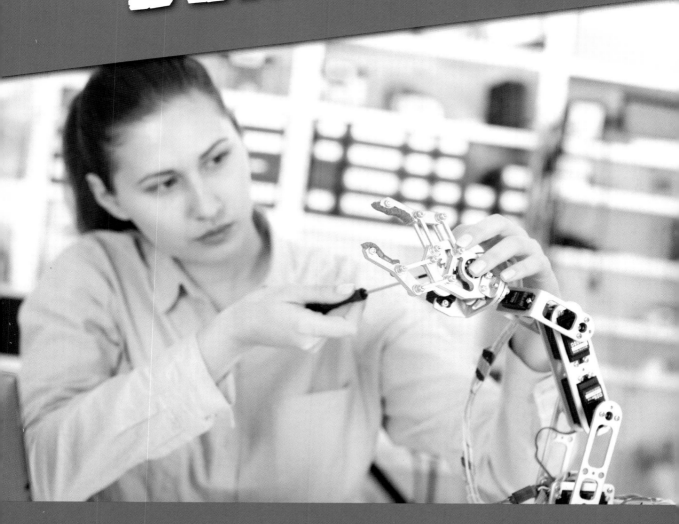

KEVIN CUNNINGHAM

Published in the United States of America by Cherry Lake Publishing
Ann Arbor, Michigan
www.cherrylakepublishing.com

Content Adviser: Chris Marcus, Esys Automation
Reading Adviser: Marla Conn, ReadAbility, Inc.

Photo Credits: © science photo/Shutterstock Images, cover, 1, 16; © Paul Fleet/Shutterstock Images, 5; Courtesy
of NASA, 6; © RAGMA IMAGES/Shutterstock Images, 9; © VARIOS GDA Photo Service/Newscom, 10;
© Joyfuldesigns | Dreamstime.com - FIRST Science And Technology Teen Competition Photo, 13; © svetikd/iStock
Images, 14; © Monkey Business Images/Shutterstock Images, 15; © Minerva Studio/Shutterstock Images, 19;
© Alessandrozocc | Dreamstime.com - Stephen Hawking Photo, 20; © RGB Ventures/SuperStock/Alamy, 22;
© ABB Group, 25; © bogdanhoda/Shutterstock Images, 26; © daseaford/Shutterstock Images, 28

Library of Congress Cataloging-in-Publication Data

Cunningham, Kevin, 1966–author.
  Robot scientist/Kevin Cunningham.
    pages cm.—(Cool STEAM careers)
  Summary: "Readers will learn what it takes to succeed as a robot scientist. The book also explains the necessary
educational steps, useful character traits, potential hazards, and daily job tasks related to this career. Sidebars include
thought-provoking trivia. Questions in the backmatter ask for text-dependent analysis. Photos, a glossary, and additional
resources are included."—Provided by publisher
  Audience: Ages 8–12
  Audience: Grades 4 to 6
  Includes bibliographical references and index.
  ISBN 978-1-63362-562-4 (hardcover)—ISBN 978-1-63362-652-2 (pbk.)—ISBN 978-1-63362-742-0 (pdf)—
ISBN 978-1-63362-832-8 (ebook)
  1. Robots—Juvenile literature. 2. Robotics—Vocational guidance—Juvenile literature. I. Title. II.
Series: 21st century skills library. Cool STEAM careers.

  TJ211.2.C86 2016
  629.8'92—dc23
                            2015005363

Cherry Lake Publishing would like to acknowledge the work of
the Partnership for 21st Century Skills. Please visit *www.p21.org*
for more information.

Printed in the United States of America
Corporate Graphics

ABOUT THE AUTHOR

Kevin Cunningham is the author of 60 books, including a series on diseases in history and other
books in Cherry Lake's Global Products series. He lives near Chicago, Illinois.

TABLE OF CONTENTS

STEAM is the acronym for Science, Technology, Engineering, Arts, and Mathematics. In this book, you will read about how each of these study areas is connected to a career in robotics.

CHAPTER 1

FAKE AND REAL

The crowd poured out of the movie theater. Maria and Steve wore wide smiles. For the past two hours, they had watched **robots** fly through space, fight crime, make jokes, and save the world.

Their dad led them to the bus stop. They joined a long line of people waiting for the bus.

"We need a giant robot to fly us home," Maria said.

"Can you build one, Dad?" Steve asked.

Their father worked in a robot laboratory. He laughed at the question. "Robots can do incredible things," he explained. "Right now, though, we haven't quite invented the giant, flying kind."

"What kinds are there?" Maria asked.

Their father ticked off answers on his fingers. "Robots that work. Robots that explore. Robots that help the military. All kinds. Just not giant ones that give us rides."

Rain began to fall.

"That's too bad," Steve said.

Many kinds of robots already exist—but some are still in people's imaginations.

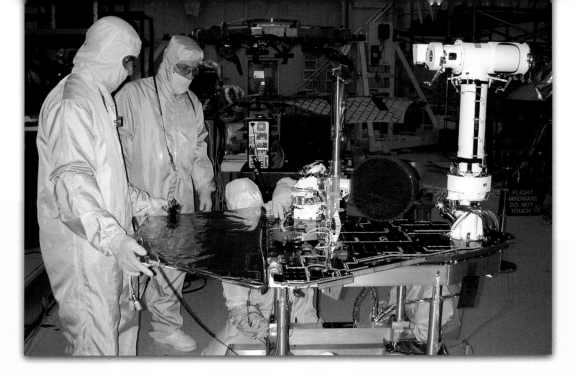

This robot belongs to the National Aeronautics and Space Administration, known as NASA.

Smart, complex, and even dangerous robots have entertained us for almost 100 years. In fact, the Czech writer Karel Capek coined the word *robot* for a stage play in 1921. Today, robot characters appear in all kinds of roles in movies and video games and on television. The inflatable robot Baymax in *Big Hero 6* cares for the sick and hurt. In *Pacific Rim*, giant robot warriors battle alien monsters that rise out of the sea.

Scientists have yet to build robots with true **artificial intelligence**, but many robots are able to help humans by exploring shipwrecks and roaming the surface of Mars. Doctors have even begun to send tiny robots into our bodies to look for problems. Robots can also do chores like vacuuming, and other things that are easy for humans but very repetitive.

Without a doubt, tomorrow's robot scientists will keep taking the human-robot partnership in amazing new directions.

THINK ABOUT ART

In 2013, artist Ryan Kiessling worked on an unusual project. With two robot partners, he created drawings in three different cities at the same time. Kiessling drew a face on a piece of canvas in Vienna, Austria. A sensor traced his pen's movements. Robots in London and Berlin received signals from the sensor via satellite and copied Kiessling's every move. Afterward, Kiessling showed the three drawings together in museums.

CHAPTER 2

THE FIRST ROBOTS

Scientists and inventors have experimented with robots since ancient times. Archytas, a Greek mathematician, built a robotic bird named the Pigeon around 400 BCE.

The Arab scientist and inventor Al-Jazari worked in what is now Turkey in the mid- and late 1100s. He invented an elephant-shaped water clock and a hand-washing device, but Al-Jazari made history with his robotic machines. He built moving peacocks and four robot musicians that played for guests at royal parties.

People have been designing robots for hundreds of years.

The genius Leonardo da Vinci drew up plans for a robot in the 1490s. Da Vinci imagined a human-shaped robot wearing armor like a knight. According to his plans, a system of cables and pulleys would have allowed the robot to sit up, move its arms and legs, turn its head, and raise its mask.

In the 1700s, Jacques de Vaucanson turned robots into a successful entertainment business. His Flute Player, made of wood, could perform a dozen songs. Crowds in Paris paid to see and hear it play. Vaucanson topped

Some robots are built to function underwater.

[21ST CENTURY SKILLS LIBRARY]

himself with the Digesting Duck. The size of an actual duck, the machine thrilled audiences by flapping its wings, quacking, eating and drinking, and pooping.

The next century, Tanaka Hisashige constructed robotic machines called karakuri dolls to entertain the rich and powerful of Japan. Other works like clocks and steam-powered engines led him to start a company that later became part of modern-day Toshiba.

THINK ABOUT ENGINEERING

All machines need power in order to work. A toaster draws on electricity. A car engine uses gasoline. Engineers must figure out a robot's power source. Today's robots most often use electricity. Electrical cables feed robots in factories. Batteries charged by electricity power Nereus, a robot vehicle that explores the deepest parts of the ocean. Opportunity, a robot rolling around Mars, recharges its batteries with solar energy.

Today's Robot Creators

Early robot makers used a process called trial and error. With trial and error, people experiment with different ideas until they hit on the right one. Robot builders today, though, can use plans worked out by earlier scientists and engineers if they choose. Students who attend camps that teach the basic elements of building robots benefit from this kind of earlier work.

Robotics have also become a popular hobby. Companies sell kits that allow the owner to build a robotic arm, a walking robot, a vehicle, or insect-sized

Many high schools have competitive robotics teams.

"bug bots." Robotics clubs have popped up in cities and towns. Members meet to show off their robots, share tips and news, and have fun.

People who create robots for a living started out by taking math and science in high school. From there, they went to college for classes in math, logic, computer science, physics, and engineering. Many finished with a degree in engineering or math. During college, they may have worked as part of a robot creation team.

Robot scientists need to have very strong computer skills.

More U.S. universities than ever offer students a chance to work with robots. The world-famous CSAIL Center for Robotics makes the Massachusetts Institute of Technology (MIT) a leader in the field. Several other robotics labs also call MIT home. Robot scientists can also find great opportunities at the Robotics Institute at Carnegie Mellon University and the Institute for Robotics and Intelligent Machines at Georgia Tech.

Combining a good education with hands-on training opens the door to jobs in companies, with the government, or on staff at a university or college. Many people start their own robotics business.

No matter where a robot scientist works, he or she starts on a new project by talking to the people who will work with the robot. These people explain what the robot needs to do and where it will work. Important questions like the robot's cost and size, and what

People working together on a robot need to communicate their ideas well.

Robots are almost always based on prototypes.

materials go into building it, depend on the robot's purpose. A robot built to jump into a mine shaft needs to be tough. One designed to light up for babies cannot have small parts or sharp edges.

Once a robot scientist has answers, plans are drawn up. Other designers, and maybe consumers, keep making suggestions. In the end, the plans go through many changes before a creator declares them finished. The scientist and his or her team turn the plans into a **prototype**. This is a first attempt at building the bot. A prototype gives the scientist a chance to see if the machine will work. It often takes several prototypes to get it right. Workers then build a robot or robots based on the prototype.

Some robot scientists use simulation software. Before they ask a robot to try a task, they use the software to check if it's even possible to be completed.

Now the robot scientist must test the machine to make sure it works. If the robot develops a problem later on, its owner will ask the builder to come in and fix it.

THINK ABOUT MATH

MoMath, the Museum of Mathematics in New York City, opened a new exhibit called Robot Swarm in 2014. In the exhibit, four sock-footed people stepped onto a square floor with several Frisbee-sized robots. In modes like "Run Away," "Pursue," and "Swarm," the robots reacted to the visitors' movements. Each robot was wearing a camera beneath its body. The cameras were connected to a coordinates system via Wi-Fi. Then a master computer told it how to move. The exhibits' creators used a type of math called **geometry** to make it all work.

ROBOTS FOR OUR HEALTH

Robots have many responsibilities in hospitals, from performing important operations to carrying medicine. In 2014, a robot equipped with a special light patrolled a Dallas hospital, zapping the deadly disease Ebola.

Surgeons once needed to cut open a person to investigate serious medical problems. Today, medical robots slip through a very small cut to get inside the body. Such machines can enter veins and even the heart. The surgeon, meanwhile, sits at a monitor that shows images blown up to large size. By using the robot as eyes, the doctor gets a clear picture of what's going on inside a patient without having to perform a major operation.

This robot can help doctors test patients' blood.

Astrophysicist Stephen Hawking is disabled, but his robotic wheelchair allows him to "speak" by moving his face slightly.

As for major operations, robots have begun to assist in that area, too. By the end of 2014, more than 2,000 da Vinci Surgical Systems operated in U.S. hospitals. The da Vinci holds tools such as scissors or knives (called scalpels) in its four hands. A surgeon moves the robot's arms and hands with computer controls. The robot's hands can move in ways the human hand cannot.

THINK ABOUT TECHNOLOGY

Someday soon, your doctor may ask you to swallow a tiny robot at your annual checkup. These robots, equipped with a camera and able to crawl, will travel down your throat, into your stomach, and through your intestines. The doctor, meanwhile, will study the images from the camera to spot problems or danger signs. Will the machine live inside your body forever? No. After the checkup, the robot will just pass out of your system with body waste.

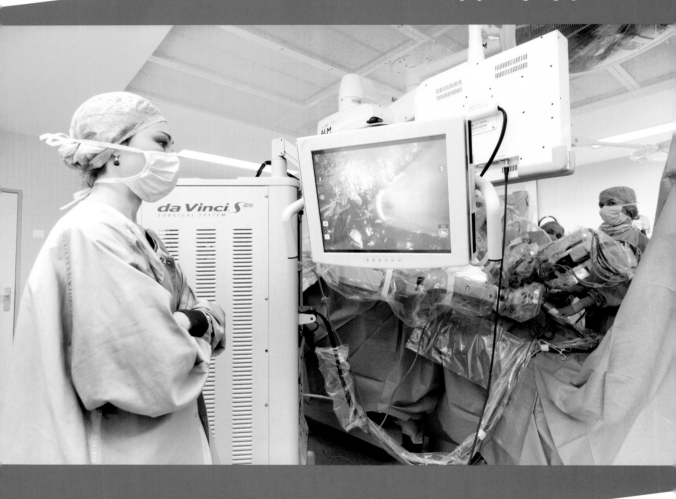

This da Vinci robot is performing surgery.

[21ST CENTURY SKILLS LIBRARY]

The computer also adjusts the movement of its hands if the surgeon's hand slips or shakes.

The da Vinci cannot operate without human control. One of its advantages is that it allows a surgeon to work inside the patient through a small opening. That reduces pain and helps the patient recover more quickly.

Robots help doctors provide care to people far away. By operating robotic arms over the Internet, a surgeon in Kansas City can save a life in Vancouver. Physicians call it **remote surgery**. Experts believe that in the future, physicians may use remote surgery to treat soldiers wounded on battlefields or accident victims who need a special kind of surgeon not available on the scene. Similar **technology** lets doctors examine and talk to patients who live far away from hospitals or clinics.

CHAPTER 5

ROBOTS AT WORK

George Devol had an idea. Actually, he had more than one. By 1954, he had already worked on inventions like radar, an early microwave oven, and automatic doors. That year, he finished designing Unimate, a robot worker. Devol teamed with engineer Joseph F. Engelberger to start a robotics company to make copies of Unimate. The first Unimate bot began to work with car parts at a General Motors factory in 1961 in New Jersey. Today, thousands of working robots—called **industrial** robots—build cars and trucks for automakers around the world.

According to the International Federation of Robotics, companies sold about 168,000 robots in 2013. These machines make everything from computer chips to sandwiches.

Companies use robots for jobs that humans consider boring or dangerous.

Robots are often used in factories, to help with manufacturing.

[21ST CENTURY SKILLS LIBRARY]

Three things keep industrial robots from being even more popular. First, robots create safety problems. Their weight, strength, and clumsiness present dangers to human workers. Second, setting up a robot takes a lot of training. Few people can do the job. Third, even an inexpensive industrial robot costs as much as a new car.

THINK ABOUT SCIENCE

Robots that explore caves or dive into the ocean help scientists understand the natural world. But robots play a role in learning about the science of other planets, too. After a 33.9 million-mile (54.5 million kilometer) journey, a pair of robots arrived on Mars in January 2004. Scientists sent these **rovers,** named Spirit and Opportunity, on a 90-day mission to look for proof of water, study Martian rocks, and see if the planet might support life. The robots surprised everyone by lasting far longer than 90 days. Spirit worked for six years before it stopped working! As of early 2015, Opportunity was still sending back information and photos. The robots fulfilled their mission. Thanks to their help, we know much more about the red planet.

Robot scientists work to solve these problems. To make industrial robots safer, they use lighter and cheaper materials like plastic, and they keep the machines small. Engineers, meanwhile, develop ways to allow people with less training to set up and fix the machines. Such improvements also lower the cost of a robot.

Some factories even use collaborative robots, or robots that can work alongside people, doing the same job. A robot like this has safety controls that allow other workers to stand next to it and even nudge it over if it's in their way. It's like having a coworker with superhuman powers.

With the hard work of engineers and robot scientists, robots will play more of a role in everyday life as the years go by.

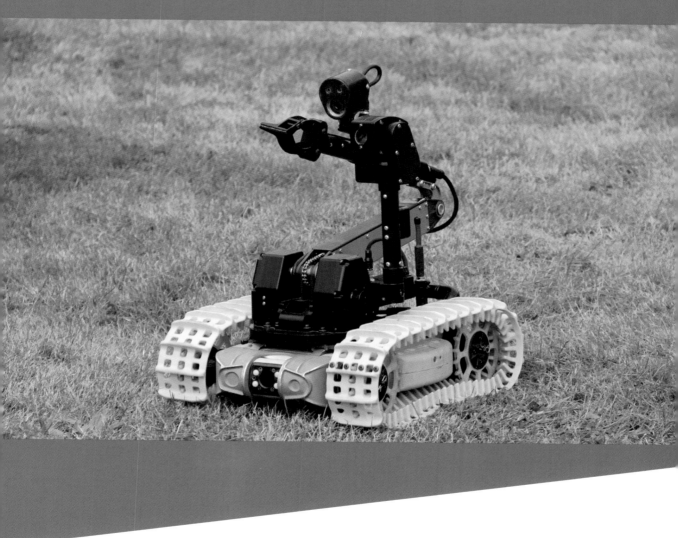

This remote-controlled robot is used to get rid of bombs safely.

THINK ABOUT IT

Think about one of your favorite hobbies—maybe it's playing music or a certain sport, or making crafts. Then try to come up with a plan for a robot that could help you do this activity. Share your idea with a parent or teacher, and write down more details. Maybe you can even build it!

Go online and look for examples of robots that didn't work the way their inventors expected. (Try going on YouTube and searching for "robot fails.") Take one example and see if you can come up with a way to improve the design.

Choose two modern inventions that you use at home. Write down some guesses about how they were invented. Go online to see if you're right. Are there any robotic elements to these objects? How do you think they will improve in the future? What are the similarities and differences between how these two objects were made?

LEARN MORE

FURTHER READING

Brasch, Nicolas. *Robots of the Future*. New York: PowerKids Press, 2012.

Ceceri, Kathy. *Robotics: Discover the Science and Technology of the Future with 20 Projects*. White River Junction, VT: Nomad Press, 2012.

Clay, Kathryn. *Humanoid Robots: Running into the Future*. North Mankato, MN: Capstone, 2014.

Mercer, Bobby. *The Robot Book: Build & Control 20 Electric Gizmos, Moving Machines, and Hacked Toys*. Chicago: Chicago Review Press, 2014.

Rusch, Elizabeth. *The Mighty Mars Rovers: The Incredible Adventures of Spirit and Opportunity*. New York: HMH for Young Readers, 2012.

Schutten, Jan Paul. *Hello from 2030: The Science of the Future and You*. New York: Aladdin/Beyond Worlds, 2014.

WEB SITES

Botball
www.botball.org
Botball is a competition that teaches robot-building skills to teams of students.

FIRST
www.usfirst.org
This group encourages the development of students' science, engineering, and technology skills.

MoMath
http://momath.org/home/robot-swarm
Read more about the *Robot Swarm* exhibit at the Museum of Mathematics.

GLOSSARY

artificial intelligence (ahr-tuh-FISH-uhl in-TEL-i-juhns) the science of making computers do things that previously needed human intelligence, such as understanding language

geometry (jee-AH-meh-tree) a type of math that deals with shapes, lines, and points

industrial (in-DUHS-tree-uhl) having to do with factories and making products in large quantities

prototype (PROH-tuh-tipe) the first working model

remote surgery (ree-MOTE SUR-jur-ee) an operation performed by a doctor who controls a robot from far away

robotics (roh-BAH-tiks) the science of creating robots

robots (ROH-bahts) machines that operate on their own or by remote control

rovers (ROH-verz) space vehicles designed to land on and explore planets; these robots were sent by the United States to the planet Mars

technology (tek-NOL-uh-jee) the use of science to make products

INDEX